THE PYRAMID PLOT

Justin Somper

Designed and illustrated by Peter Wingham

Cover design: Russell Punter
Front cover illustration: Christyan Fox

Series editor: Gaby Waters
Assistant editor: Rachael Robinson

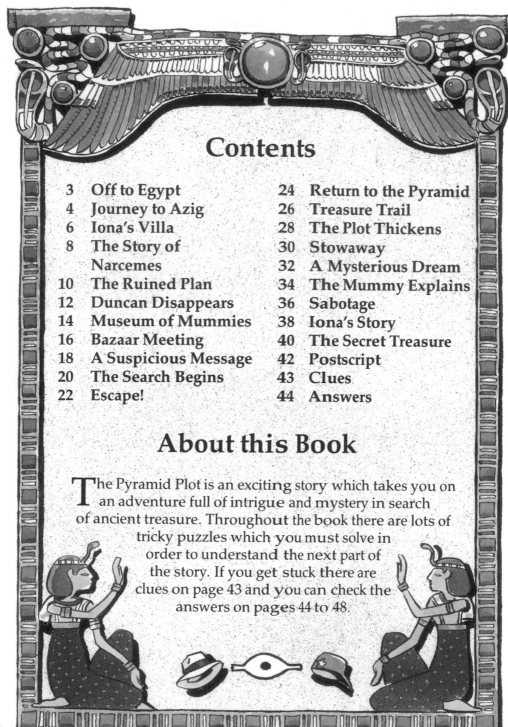

Contents

About this Book

The Pyramid Plot is an exciting story which takes you on an adventure full of intrigue and mystery in search of ancient treasure. Throughout the book there are lots of tricky puzzles which you must solve in order to understand the next part of the story. If you get stuck there are clues on page 43 and you can check the answers on pages 44 to 48.

Off to Egypt

Gusto fastened her seat-belt as the plane began its descent. Jaz rummaged in his backpack for the letter and newspaper clipping from their dad. Soon they would see him again – in Egypt of all places!

> ... a final word from your captain... I hope you've had a pleasant flight. It's a sunny 28 degrees in Egypt today and the local time is 10.45.

Gusto Ffax

Jaz Ffax

February 19th — The Egyptian Inquirer

FORTUNE KEEPS ON SMILING

Iona Fortune: "... passionately interested"

by ace reporter Boz Babbleboy

The lovely Iona Fortune, widow of tycoon Ronald, has reason to smile! She may be on course for the archaeological coup of the century – the treasures stolen over four thousand years ago from the tomb of Pharaoh Narcemes IV.

Moving to Egypt three months ago, Ms Fortune told the Enquirer, "I need to make a fresh start. I've always been passionately interested in civil engineering, so I decided to settle close by the Aswan dam."

The divine Ms F bought a prime piece of land, close to the Nile and in the shadow of Narcemes' pyramid, where she planned to build a luxurious villa.

Shortly after construction work began, a small but important cache of treasure was unearthed. "I've always been passionately interested in archaeology," Ms F tells the Enquirer. "I knew at once that I'd found Narcemes' stolen treasures."

Ms F immediately called in Kuri Osites, Minister of Ancient Bits and Pieces, who declared the site an official excavation zone. "I don't want to make any lavish promises."

Kuri Osites: "sitting on a goldmine"

Mr Osites tells us, "But, yes, we could be sitting on a goldmine."

With Ms Fortune's generous assistance, Mr Osites contacted famed archaeologist Arty Ffax to organize the dig. So far, the findings have been slim, but Ffax remains hopeful. "The treasures were buried four thousand years ago. An awful lot of sand's been blown about since then."

Ms Fortune was forced to abandon plans to build a villa at the site of the dig. At great personal cost, she found another location where construction of a new villa is almost complete.

Arty Ffax: "an awful lot of sand"

JAILBREAK!

The cheeky conman known as Bricabrac has broken free from Oriac Prison. Warden Intha Klink expressed sorrow at the escape. "He really seemed to be making an effort to go straight this time. He was even taking a class in woodwork and basic building skills." Readers are advised not to approach Bricabrac, unless they wish to lose large sums of money and personal possessions.

Des Res Properties Inc.

For the crème de la crème of properties on the Egyptian Riviera... four hour service with a ... Azig 300 or Oriac ... ed at 145. The ... me for a

Villa Fortuna
Near Azig
Egypt

Feb 21st

Dear Gusto and Jaz,

When you get to the airport, take the bus to the harbour and catch the boat to Azig — there's one a day at noon. Someone will meet you there — I'll leave a note at the airport with all the details. Can't wait to see you!

Love,

Dad xx

PS Thought you'd like to see this newspaper clipping all about the dig.

PPS Love to your mother and thanks for the socks she knitted me for Christmas.

Journey to Azig

Jaz and Gusto stumbled out of the crowded bus and fell in a heap on to the bustling dockside. The sun was scorching and the air was stifling, but it felt great to be in Egypt.

Gusto stretched out, happy just taking in the strange new sights and sounds, but Jaz was eager to get going. The boat to Azig would be leaving any minute now. There was no time to lose...

Half an hour later, the twins were cruising down the river Nile on the top deck of a crowded steamer bound for the ancient town of Azig. Jaz pulled out his camera and started snapping away furiously.

Gusto waved at the feluccas sailing silently past and wondered what the coming week held in store. She was looking forward to seeing her dad again and couldn't wait to find out more about his new dig.

At last Azig harbour came into view. Gusto glanced at her watch – the boat was only half an hour late. Jaz delved into his pocket and retrieved the note his dad had left for them at the airport.

Their dad's new assistant was supposed to be meeting them, but there was a huge crowd milling at the water's edge. He wasn't going to be easy to spot.

Can you find him?

5

Iona's Villa

Duncan led them away from the crowded harbour towards a red jeep parked in a side street. They heaved their bags into the back while Duncan jumped behind the wheel.

"We're all staying at Iona's new villa," Duncan explained as they bumped along the highway. "It was Iona who first discovered the treasure, buried in the sand just where she planned to build her villa, a stone's throw away from the pyramid."

"Now your dad and I are excavating the site," Duncan continued, as they headed into the desert. "And Iona has built a brand new villa on another site, way over there."

"Will you excavate the pyramid as well?" asked Jaz as they passed the great stone edifice itself.

"Oh dear me no," chortled Duncan, accelerating suddenly. "That was done more than a hundred years ago by Inigo Outicombe, the great Victorian archaeologist."

On and on they drove along the desert road until at last a dazzling white building, surrounded by palm trees, came into sight. This had to be Iona's new villa.

The twins jumped out of the jeep into a courtyard that was in the process of being built. Duncan revved the engine and shot off without another word.

But Gusto and Jaz didn't notice for at that moment a woman looking very much like a movie star sashayed towards them in a swirl of perfume.

Iona Fortune

Do you really?

It's her name, stupid.

Iona introduced herself and said their father was waiting for them at the pyramid.

"It's a lovely little walk," she beamed, handing them a map. **Can you find the way?**

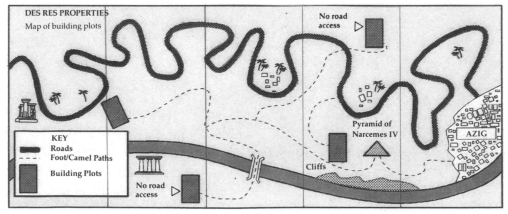

DES RES PROPERTIES
Map of building plots

No road access

No road access

Pyramid of Narcemes IV

Cliffs

AZIG

KEY
Roads
Foot/Camel Paths
Building Plots

The Story of Narcemes

After a hot and dusty walk through the desert, the twins found their dad waiting for them outside the pyramid.

"Gusto! Jaz!" he cried, lifting them off their feet. "It's great to see you. I can't wait to tell you all about the dig, but first I want to show you the pyramid."

The twins followed their dad through a narrow entrance into the pyramid along a dark passage that climbed steeply upwards. At the end they stepped into a huge stone chamber. In the dim half light, they could just make out the paintings and symbols that adorned the walls. This was the burial chamber of Narcemes.

This is the great Pharaoh Narcemes the fourth . . . Cheerful isn't he?

The symbols, or hieroglyphs, on these walls tell his story.

Narcemes was a strong ruler but all he cared about was his vast hoard of treasure.

Narcemes summoned his architect, Skemes, and ordered him to build this great pyramid.

When it was built, the burial chamber was in the wrong place – beneath the middle of the pyramid.

It was a simple error but the Pharaoh was furious. That was the last pyramid Skemes ever built.

Narcemes hired another architect who built a new chamber here in the middle of the pyramid.

With his pyramid complete Narcemes was a new man. A few years later he died, happy at last.

Narcemes and his riches were entombed in this room. But thieves soon broke in and stole the treasure.

Now here's a mystery. The symbols on this panel are different. No one has ever deciphered them.

The Ruined Plan

Arriving back at the villa, the twins were hungry and pleased to find that Iona had laid on a barbecue. Unfortunately, she'd left Duncan in charge. Iona introduced the twins to her friend, Kuri Osites, and advised them to have some salad.

Everyone rummaged for charred remains in the barbecue and sat down at the table. Mr Osites was full of questions about the dig, which he was helping to organize. Duncan seemed keen to say something too, but Iona kept butting in whenever he tried.

After a surprisingly delicious pudding of camel's milk ice cream and desert berries, Iona dashed inside. Duncan jumped up and spread a roll of paper across the table.

Iona reappeared, clutching a bottle of purple liquid. She seemed very surprised to see the plan. As she rushed over, she lost her balance and dropped the bottle.

The strange smelling purple liquid soaked the antique plan. Iona tried her best to save it, but it was no use. She scrunched the plan up, tore it into several pieces and threw it away.

Later, as Kuri said goodbye, the twins' dad started to recite a terrible old poem. Gusto and Jaz were wondering how to shut him up when they felt a firm hand on their shoulders.

Startled, they spun round to find Duncan uttering a dire warning.

Duncan scuttled away. Jaz and Gusto turned to one another, aghast.

As they struggled to make sense of Duncan's warning, Iona and their dad disappeared inside. The twins glanced sadly at the plan. It was beyond repair . . . or was it?

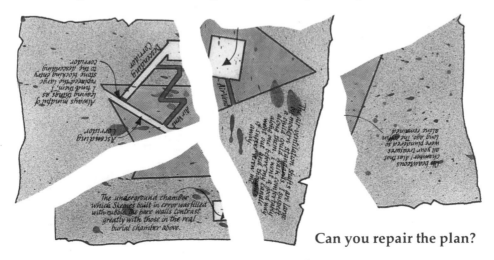

Can you repair the plan?

Duncan Disappears

Gusto and Jaz were up and about early the next morning. Just before eight they raced downstairs, eager to keep their rendezvous with Duncan and find out what he had meant by his strange warning.

Dear Gypsy and Buzz,
Darlings, I'm zipping off to Oriac to do some shopping. Your father's made an early start at the dig. If you want to visit him, why not take Cleo, my Arabian mare.
Catch you later
Iona

The table on the terrace had been laid for breakfast, but no one was around. The red jeep had gone and there was no sign of Iona. Then Jaz spied a note, neatly tucked in the toast rack. He picked it up and began to read.

Ten minutes later, Duncan had still not appeared, so the twins decided to investigate. The door to his room was shut. Jaz knocked but there was no reply. He pushed the door. The room was empty.

The twins went inside. At once, Gusto noticed Duncan's notebook lying open, face down on the floor. She picked it up and flipped through the pages. The final page of writing had been torn out, and judging by the tear, it had been done in a hurry.

What did this mean? Where was Duncan? What had happened? They sprinted to the stables and found Cleo. In a flash, they saddled her up and set off for the excavation site at a gallop. Maybe their dad would have some of the answers.

The twins found their dad in a hut looking at some bits of a broken pot. He didn't seem very worried about Duncan and started to show them his latest discoveries.

All of a sudden, Jaz felt a tremendous sneeze coming on. As it erupted, he fell back, knocking an ancient jar to the floor. Gusto gasped as it shattered but her dad was silent.

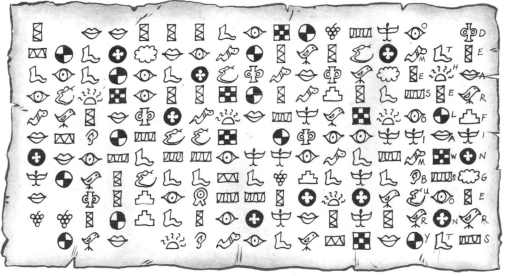

Amongst the shattered fragments was a roll of frayed papyrus. Their dad carefully unfurled the scroll. It was covered with hieroglyphs which someone had started to translate.

Intrigued, the twins soon realized that they could complete the job.

Can you decipher the hieroglyphics?

Museum of Mummies

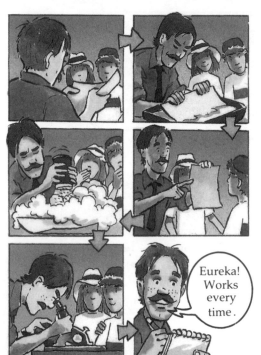

A letter from one of the pyramid thieves! An amazing find – if it was genuine.

"We can soon find out by dating it," said the twins' dad, dipping the letter into a clear solution. It turned blue. He lifted it out, sprinkled some powder on it and slipped it into a device like a microscope, twiddling various cogs.

"2264 BC!" he announced at last. "That's the year Narcemes died. The letter is genuine."

"We'll make an archaeologist of you yet!" he beamed, patting Jaz on the head, proudly.

Jaz was thinking about what the thief had written. If he was telling the truth, then most of Narcemes' treasure was buried somewhere else, perhaps still undiscovered. Jaz couldn't wait to learn more about Narcemes and the missing treasure. But where should they begin?

An hour later, Gusto and Jaz stood inside the Museum of Mummies at Oriac, facing a row of brightly painted coffins. X-rays showed the mummies inside. But which was Narcemes? There were no labels, so the twins asked a guide for help.

Which is Narcemes' coffin?

Narcemes IV? Certainly. Turn to face them and he's left of Scesamby and right of Narcemes III. Speoch's the one on the left of Numaknatuth, the boy king. Kinpiah's to the right of Netahenka I, who's the one to the right of Samres VI. Petonemah is to the right of Scesamby and on the left of Speoch. Numaknatuth is on the left of Ites who's on the left of Samres VI. OK?

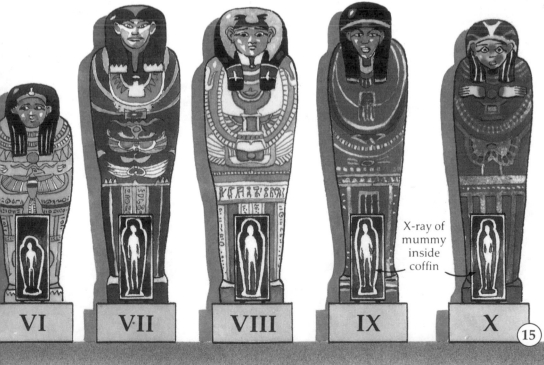

X-ray of mummy inside coffin

VI   VII   VIII   IX   X

Bazaar Meeting

Wandering away from the museum, the twins soon found themselves in the sticky throng of the bazaar. Something was bugging Jaz – something he'd seen that didn't quite make sense. But whatever it was, was firmly stuck at the back of his mind.

It was time to catch the bus back to Azig. He called to Gusto, but his voice was drowned out by the din. Besides, she seemed to have spotted a friend.

Gusto tapped Kuri on the arm. He spun round looking flustered. Gusto apologized. She hadn't meant to frighten him, or interrupt his conversation with a woman wearing dark glasses.

The woman introduced herself and explained that she had fainted in the heat of the bazaar and Kuri had brought her round with the kiss of life. Kuri looked rather sheepish.

"What you need is a sun-hat!" exclaimed Gusto, grabbing Miss Favisham and dragging her through the crowd to a hat stall.

Jaz and Kuri watched as Gusto grabbed a large hat and plonked it on to Miss Favisham's head. It looked awful.

Gusto tossed it away and tried another. Jaz and Kuri shook their heads. This one was worse. As Gusto yanked at the hat, Miss Favisham looked very cross and Jaz noticed something odd.

What has Jaz noticed?

A Suspicious Message

Jaz seized Gusto's hand and tugged her away, blurting to Kuri that they had a bus to catch. Gusto was puzzled, but when Jaz told her what he'd seen, she was even more puzzled. Things were getting stranger by the minute. What ever would happen next?

Turning the next corner, feeling very confused, Gusto spotted the bus bound for Azig and they set off at a sprint.

Later, as the twins climbed the path up to the villa, the sound of voices and laughter drifted over the garden wall. Gusto scrambled on to Jaz's shoulders to take a look.

Brushing aside some leaves to get a better view, Gusto found Iona's builders having a tea break. Nothing unusual about that, but their conversation was very curious...

Back inside the villa, the twins were surprised to find Iona coolly mixing cocktails. Jaz asked if Duncan had returned.

"No," replied his dad, shaking his head. "And I'm starting to worry. It's not like him to go off without leaving a note."

Silly me! I saw it on Duncan's bedside table this morning but I didn't think to pick it up.

With a gasp, Iona dropped the cocktail shaker and darted out of the room. She was back in a trice, waving an envelope which she handed to the twins' dad.

He tore it open and read with relief the letter inside. The twins, reading over his shoulder, felt quite sick.

Why are the twins concerned?

Dear Arty,
   HI! EVErything's OK. A friend introduced me to some bElgian tourists planning a trip down thE nile and seeKing a knowledgeable guide. i coulD certaiNly do with the cAsh! I know it's not the best time to disaPpear. perhaps Jaz and Gusto can lEnD you a Hand while I'm gonE. I shouLd be back in a couPle of days.

   Duncan

The Search Begins

G usto and Jaz needed to talk things over, alone. But first they had to eat the lavish dinner prepared by Iona.

Seven courses of strange delicacies later, they finally made their escape and sloped off upstairs yawning loudly.

In hushed voices, they discussed their suspicions. Then they decided to start by making a search of the villa for clues.

 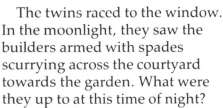

The twins raced to the window. In the moonlight, they saw the builders armed with spades scurrying across the courtyard towards the garden. What were they up to at this time of night?

In a flash, Gusto remembered the curious conversation she'd overheard earlier and began to think. Could they be involved in the strange goings on at the villa? There was only one way to find out.

They spent the next few hours solidly sleuthing. By midnight, they had yet to find a clue that would lead them to Duncan or any incriminating evidence that would prove Iona was involved.

Only the room next to their own remained unexplored but the door was locked. Jaz was about to force his way in when he was startled by the sound of breaking glass and voices outside.

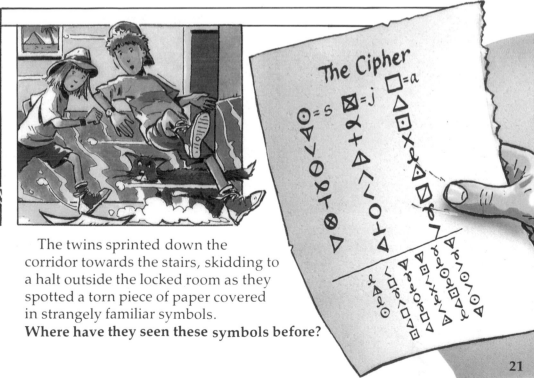

The twins sprinted down the corridor towards the stairs, skidding to a halt outside the locked room as they spotted a torn piece of paper covered in strangely familiar symbols.

Where have they seen these symbols before?

Escape!

Jaz shoved the sheet of paper into his pocket as they raced towards the stairs. There wasn't time to wonder where it had come from, for just as they were about to slide down the bannisters, Iona sprang out of the shadows.

"I thought you were in bed," said Iona. "Can't you sleep? Perhaps you'd like a nightcap?"

The twins shook their heads, yawned loudly and beat a hasty retreat.

I didn't like the sound of Iona's nightcap.

Get knotting!

Girls first.

Jaz was ready for bed, but Gusto was keen to get back on the trail of the builders. They just had to find a way out of the villa without alerting Iona. Suddenly, Gusto began tearing the sheets off her bed.

Jaz helped Gusto knot all their sheets together into a sort of rope, then they looped one end firmly around the foot of Gusto's bed and tossed the rest of the line out of the window. It was a long drop to the ground.

One at a time, the twins clambered eagerly down their makeshift rope and made straight for the stables, hoping to enlist Cleo's help in pursuing the builders.

Cleo seemed to sense that her finest hour was at hand. Gusto swung into the saddle followed by Jaz and without delay the mare raced off down the garden towards the back gates.

Moments later, they were out of the grounds and heading into the open desert. But the builders had disappeared.

They would never be able to follow them now . . . or would they? **Can you work out how to follow the builders?**

Return to the Pyramid

Moonlight flickered through the branches overhead as Cleo raced towards her unknown destination.

Gusto was sure they were on to something . . . Iona had kidnapped Duncan and forced him to type the note to throw their dad off the scent. But why? Was it connected with the search for Narcemes' treasure? Where did the builders fit in? Were they Iona's flunkies or had they their own rotten scheme?

Jaz shivered with cold and wondered if this wasn't all a wild goose chase. Maybe the builders were just doing a spot of overtime. But then he looked up. Wasn't that the pyramid in the distance? Yes, and there was someone going inside!

The twins slipped out of the saddle and tethered Cleo to an abandoned souvenir stall. Then, careful not to make a sound, they stole through the shadows to the entrance of the pyramid.

Moving cautiously up to the entrance, the twins heard voices echoing faintly from somewhere deep within the pyramid. As they stepped inside, Jaz snapped off his torch. The passage led straight to the burial chamber. They couldn't risk being seen.

As they crept up the passage, the voices seemed to grow fainter. Gusto was trying to figure this out when she walked into a pillar.

Jaz flicked on his torch. They were in the burial chamber, but it was empty. So where had the voices come from? Had their ears tricked them? Jaz shone his torch on the walls. As he stared at the strange symbols, he remembered his dad's words the last time they looked at this small stone panel. Reaching into his pocket, he pulled out the piece of paper they'd found outside the locked room.

Can you translate the hieroglyphics?

Treasure Trail

Hiho, Hiho, I'll never work again . . .

What did Narcemes' riddle mean? Gusto struggled to make sense of what the middle might be, when they suddenly heard a familiar voice coming from somewhere below. They stumbled back down the passage in darkness.

At the end of the passage they stopped abruptly. Taking shelter in the shadows, they watched in silent amazement as Bricabrac and his troop of pals appeared through a hole in the wall, their arms piled high with glittering treasure.

As the builders staggered out of the pyramid, the twins took a look at the wall. Instantly, they saw that a huge stone slab had been removed to reveal a secret passage plunging down into the darkness. Just then, they heard a jeep revving up.

The twins agreed to come back and explore later. Outside, they saw the crooks heading for the river. Gusto was keen to follow, but Jaz refused to leave Cleo stranded in the desert. They would have to split up.

From the top of the cliff, Gusto watched Bricabrac and his mates load their loot into a barge roped to a felucca. As they climbed up to the jeep to collect the rest of their bounty she decided she must get aboard somehow.

Can you find a safe route down the cliff and on to the barge?

The Plot Thickens

Reaching the stall where he'd left Cleo, Jaz had a shock. The mare had gone. Had she somehow freed herself, or had someone given her a helping hand?

Jaz stared at the fresh trail of Cleo's hoofprints when suddenly the jeep zoomed past. Jaz jumped back, just in time to see one of the builders at the wheel.

Where was he heading in such a hurry? It hardly mattered now. With Cleo gone, he had no hope of following. He sighed and turned away.

Jaz sat down on a prickly mound of sand, glumly thinking about the long walk back to Iona's villa.

Suddenly, the ground began to move. This was getting ridiculous. On top of everything else – an earthquake!

The tremor was over in seconds and Jaz was still on the mound, but he seemed to be higher up than before.

Then he realized. This was no earthquake. He'd just sat down on a dozing camel. What luck! The jeep was long gone but it had left deep tracks in its wake which Caesar, for this appeared to be the camel's name, could follow.

Caesar followed the tracks to the site of the dig where they led up to the hut and away again. The crook must have stopped off here, but why? Jaz clambered down and ran over to the hut. The door was padlocked.

Fortunately, Jaz was carrying the key his dad had given him. He unlocked the door and went inside. He searched from floor to ceiling, looking for signs of recent disruption.

Nothing seemed to be missing or even disturbed. Jaz was puzzled. If the builder hadn't taken anything, why had he come?

Do you know?

Stowaway

Gusto was starting to think she'd been a bit rash hiding herself in the barge. It was hot and cramped under the tarpaulin and she felt rather queasy. She was in dire need of some air.

She wriggled along to the end of the barge and felt for the edge of the tarpaulin. As luck would have it, there was a tear in the cloth just large enough for Gusto to poke her head through.

Hmmmm. That felt better. She took a deep breath rather loudly. As she did so, one of the builders turned around.

He clambered to the stern of the felucca followed by Bricabrac. Gusto ducked down hastily, holding her breath.

She waited several minutes and looked out again. The builders were talking. Gusto strained her ears to listen in.

Piecing together the snatches of conversation, Gusto soon figured out that the builders were taking the treasure to Oriac. Here they were going to pick up something for Iona and bring it back again.

Gusto couldn't make out who was in charge of this operation – Iona, Bricabrac or a Mr Rousike, whoever he might be. But one thing was certain. They were working together.

As Oriac harbour came into view, Gusto hid herself in a spare sheet of oilcloth. Moments later, the builders rolled back the tarpaulin and unloaded the barge.

As Bricabrac greeted the mysterious Mr Rousike, Gusto risked a peep. Something about him was familiar.
Can you work out who he is?

A Mysterious Dream

Meanwhile, Jaz and Caesar arrived back at the stables. The camel was too tall to fit inside, so Jaz went to fetch him a blanket and some water. A surprise lay in wait. Cleo was asleep in the hay.

. . . Skemes put the burial chamber in the wrong place . . .

. . . thieves broke in and the treasures were never seen again until . . .

. . . not much cop. Someone must've beaten us to the good stuff . . .

There's something very wrong here. I'll be kidnapped in the morning.

Not any more. Tee hee.

It's all mine!

Do you like my nightcap?

Wrong. It's all mine!

Riddle dee dee you can't catch me!

Deep down in the ground far under the mound? Or in the centre? We'll see . . . Remember – even a Pharaoh can change his mind!

She was still tacked up in her saddle and reins, so it looked as if she'd found her own way home. Jaz settled Caesar and then lay back on some bundles of straw. He soon drifted off to sleep and into a very peculiar dream . . .

With a jolt, Jaz awoke. The dream was fresh in his mind. Perhaps it might help him sort out some of the mystery.

Can you make any sense of the dream?

The Mummy Explains

Back at the dockside, Gusto saw Kuri's face clearly as he turned to inspect the treasure. He beamed and gave Bricabrac a wad of banknotes. Bricabrac nodded and snapped his fingers. His mates carried the loot to Kuri's car.

Then, when he thought no one was looking, he pulled a handful of treasure from his pocket and chuckled. He quickly hid it again as the others returned with a new load of sacks. Gusto ducked back down.

The builders slung the sacks into the barge and picked up the tarpaulin cover. One of them spotted the tear. Gusto froze. What could she do? There was an empty sack nearby. In the nick of time, she dived into it.

After that the felucca set sail and she must have dropped off. The next thing she knew, she was swinging backwards and forwards inside the sack, as if in mid-air.

Her strange flight came to an end with a firm thud on a hard floor. She heard a door close, a key turn and footsteps retreating. She scrambled to the end of the sack and peeped out.

She was in a strange room, filled with sacks of building supplies and . . . no, it couldn't be, but yes it was . . . a mummy sitting on the floor, moaning terribly and edging nearer . . .

On closer inspection, Gusto saw that it was no mummy but Duncan, swathed from head to toe in bandages. As she unravelled him, Duncan started to explain.

When the last of Duncan's bandages was off, Gusto scanned the room for an escape route. There was no time to lose.

She had to get to the stables and find Jaz as soon as possible.

Can you find an escape route?

Sabotage

The rising sun warmed Gusto's neck as she swung down the vine. Duncan followed her, feeling his way cautiously. Then, back on the ground, they sprinted off to the stables.

Jaz was surprised to see Duncan, but not as surprised as Duncan was to see Caesar. Gusto stroked Cleo's mane, then she sprang into the saddle and pulled on the reins.

"Where are we going now?" asked Jaz.

"To find your dad," replied Duncan, climbing gingerly on to Caesar's back.

The motley crew set off, but they hadn't gone far when they spotted a familiar figure.

"Dad!" cried Gusto, as she and Jaz brought the animals to a halt. "What's up?"

"I've broken down," said her dad, looking cross. "There seems to be a hole in the fuel tank."

To the pyramid. Gee up, Caesar!

Sure enough, the tank was empty. The twins looked back at a trail of fuel. Was this sabotage? It was time to tell their dad everything.

Their dad was flabbergasted to hear that there was treasure inside the pyramid after all and couldn't wait to explore the new passage.

"It must lead to the underground chamber built by mistake," he said. "Why is there treasure down there?"

The builders have been busy.

When they reached the pyramid, Duncan was left to tether the animals while the twins dashed off towards the entrance, followed closely behind by their dad. They could scarcely contain their excitement.

But the entrance to the passage had disappeared. In its place was a stone block. What could they do now? They'd never find the underground chamber, unless . . .

Is there another way in?

Iona's Story

I wonder why we never noticed this before.

This is a typical ante-chamber. There should be another chamber nearby where they would have put the best of the treasure...

Jaz raced up the passage searching for some sign of an air vent. At last he found it – a gap in the wall that gave way to a cramped tunnel plunging and twisting steeply downwards through the heart of the pyramid.

The tunnel led into a bigger passage and then into a small, empty chamber with bare walls. Was this where the builders had discovered all those fabulous treasures? It hardly seemed possible.

Just so, Professor. Now lead the way before I make this a family tomb.

The twins' dad was busy explaining his theory when a hairy arm grabbed him roughly by the neck. It was Bricabrac brandishing a gun.

Duncan darted in front of the twins as Bricabrac pointed the gun and released the safety catch. In vain, Duncan tried to reason with him.

As Bricabrac lifted the gun, a hand appeared from nowhere and struck him on the head. A shot was fired, but the bullet hit the wall.

For a moment there was silence. Then, through the wreath of smoke left by the shot, out stepped Iona. She eased the gun from Bricabrac's fingers, emptied the bullets on to the floor and began to explain. As Gusto listened to Iona's story she noticed something even more amazing.

When I first unearthed the treasure, I found a piece of papyrus with it. This was the cipher. I decoded the riddle in the chamber above, but what did it mean? I began to wonder...

Suppose there was no error in building the burial chamber? What if the underground chamber was no mistake? Maybe the one above was just a decoy? I had to find out!

Kuri agreed to let me excavate the underground chamber. My builders unblocked the corridor and we soon discovered the treasure hidden beneath the rubble on the ground.

We protected our discovery with our own decoy – Arty Ffax. Most of the stuff was ferried to safety in Oriac, while a few trinkets were buried at the fake excavation site.

Everything was going well until Duncan found the cipher. It was Bricabrac who suggested the kidnapping. I should never have listened to him, but I panicked. I'm very sorry.

In the beginning, I was only interested in the treasures, but you've taught me to respect the past. The treasure belongs here and I'm building a museum where it will be safe.

The Secret Treasure

Gusto pointed to the spot where the bullet had fractured the wall, revealing a chamber beyond. The gap was slight, but the old bricks had loosened. The twins cleared an opening and climbed into a secret chamber where gold and jewels still sparkled after four thousand years of darkness.

But it was the hieroglyphics which most interested the twins. The symbols matched those they had already decoded in the chamber above.

"Maybe these will finally explain the pyramid plot," said Jaz excitedly.

Do they? Can you decipher them?

INSTITUTE UNVEILED

The Eg... 19th

by ace reporter Boz Babbleboy

All's well that ends well and well, who'd have thought it would end this well? Last night at a glittering gala, Ms Iona Fortune officially opened the doors of The Fortune Institute, the magnificent museum where the treasures of Narcemes will be on permanent display.

Amongst the guests at this essential soiree, this ace reporter spied Arty Ffax, ace archaeologist, and his ace twin children, Augusta and Jasper. It was Ffax who toasted a delighted Ms Fortune "... the recovery of Narcemes' treasure owes more to Iona than anyone else ..."

Of future plans, Ms F reveals that she is off to Europe, while Ffax and his children will be enjoying the sights and sounds of Egypt for a few weeks yet.

I put it to Ms Fortune that this whole pyramid plot has changed her. Does she still plan to make a home near her beloved Aswan dam? "When did I say that? Four weeks ago? An awful lot of sand has blown about since then."

Iona Fortune: "I declare it open"

BRICABRAC BACK BEHIND BARS

In a surprise turn of events, escaped convict Bricabrac gave himself up for arrest last night. Declining to reveal where he had spent his month out of captivity, he said simply, "Freedom isn't all it's cracked up to be." Delighted warden, Intha Klink added, "I think we're really making progress now. He's even signed up for a course in archaeology!"

DES RES ... TOP

Des Res Properti... profits last night following ... building land in the ... wspaper reading ... a's new found

---

Justo and Gaz
How are you? Thanks for the photos and news cutting. Such a good idea of yours to stay on for a holiday. Glad you could make use of the villa. Italy is sheer bliss. Must dash — I have to see a man about a Fresco.

The Faxes
Villa Fortuna
Egypt

Clues

Pages 4-5
This is easy. Check Duncan's description in the note, then use your eyes.

Pages 6-7
The map shows four building plots. Only one of them can possibly be the site of Iona's new villa. The newspaper clipping on page 3 and the journey to the villa on page 6 might help you.

Pages 10-11
Trace the pieces of the plan, then fit them together.

Pages 12-13
Some of the symbols have already been deciphered. Try reading the message downwards from right to left and you should be able to fill in the gaps.

Pages 14-15
Numaknatuth is the boy king. Which is his coffin?

Pages 16-17
Look carefully at Miss Favisham's hair? Have you seen her ring before or the beauty spot on her left cheek?

Pages 18-19
There are some bad typing mistakes in Duncan's note. There are capital letters where there should be small letters and small letters where there should be capitals. Is Duncan just a bad typist or could this be deliberate?

Pages 20-21
Remember the burial chamber...

Pages 22-23
There are a lot of footprints. Do you recognize any of them? Flick back through the book and have a look.

Pages 24-25
Use the cipher on page 21. The cipher is only partly complete. Fill in the rest of the letters working downwards from right to left.

Pages 26-27
Remember that Gusto must keep out of sight of the builders and the headlights of their jeep.

Pages 28-29
Have a look just outside the hut. Do you recognize anything?

Pages 30-31
Have you seen these shoes before? What a strange name.

Pages 32-33
This is quite tricky! See if you can find the thread of the story running through the dream. Look carefully at the riddle.

Pages 34-35
You've seen this room before from the outside. Where are they?

Pages 36-37
Look back at the plan of the pyramid.

Pages 40-41
You'll need to use the cipher again.

Answers

Pages 4-5

This is Duncan.

He is the only person who fits the description. In case you were wondering, Duncan was a bit late, but the boat was even later.

Pages 6-7

The site of Iona's new villa is marked in black. The easiest route to the pyramid is along the foot/camel path marked in green.

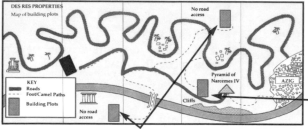

This is the site of Iona's first villa where the treasure was found. It is now the excavation site.

These building plots have no road access. Neither can be the site of Iona's new villa as Duncan drives the twins right up to the courtyard.

Pages 10-11

This is what the plan looks like when it is pieced together.

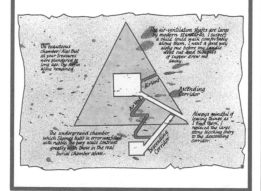

Pages 12-13

The hieroglyphics read downwards from right to left. Decoded, with spaces and punctuation marks added, this is what they say:

Dear Fingers,
The law's on to me so I'm burying this treasure wot I nicked from the pyramid of Narcemes like I told ya. It's not much cop. Someone must've beaten us to the good stuff. Anyway, see ya at the border.
Your pal,
Klepto Maniak

Pages 14-15

To find Narcemes' coffin you need to put a name to each of the Mummies.

Start with Numaknatuth, the boy king whose coffin is the smallest (number VI). The other Mummies fall into place around him. Narcemes is number II. The order of the Mummies is shown on the right:

I: Narcemes III
II: Narcemes IV
III: Scesamby
IV: Petonemah
V: Speoch
VI: Numaknatuth (the boy king)
VII: Ites
VIII: Samres VI
IX: Netahenka I
X: Kinpiah

Pages 16-17

By yanking at the hat, Gusto ruffles Miss Favisham's hair to reveal a blonde patch – this is strange as Miss Favisham is clearly dark haired. Jaz wonders if Miss Favisham is wearing a wig. Then he notices her ring and the beauty spot on her left cheek. They seem familiar. Then he remembers that he has seen them both before on Iona. Could Miss Favisham in fact be none other than Iona in disguise?

Pages 18-19

Pick out all the deliberate typing mistakes – capital letters which should be small letters and small letters which should be capitals. If you run these together in order they form a message:

I've been kidnapped. Help.

Pages 20-21

The twins have seen the symbols before in the burial chamber on page 9.

Pages 22-23

One set of footprints is familiar. Bricabrac's shoes have a star symbol on the sole.

All Gusto and Jaz need to do is follow these footprints to catch up with Bricabrac.

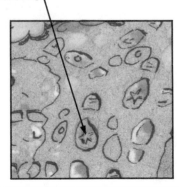

Pages 24-25

Use the cipher on page 21 to decode these symbols. The cipher only decodes the letters s, j and a. If you carry on reading down the columns, you can work out the code for the rest of the alphabet as shown below:

The symbols below the cipher form a message. Reading downwards, from right to left, they say:

This is the secret code of the Pharaoh Narcemes.

To decode the symbols on the stone panel read downwards from right to left. With spaces and punctuation marks added, this is what they say:

Here is my riddle
About the middle
And where the middle might be.
Deep down in the ground,
Far under the mound,
Or in the centre? We'll see.
Answer my riddle
And my treasure you'll find.
Remember – even a Pharaoh can change his mind.

Pages 26-27

Gusto's route is shown in red.

These are the only steps down from the top of the cliff that Gusto can reach without the risk of being spotted.

Pages 28-29

The staff half buried in the sand is identical to the one which Bricabrac was carrying out of the pyramid.

It looks as if the builder has buried it deliberately in the sand at the excavation site.

Pages 30-31

He is Kuri Osites. Gusto knows this because he is wearing exactly the same shoes as in the bazaar.

Seti Rousike is an anagram, which means that if you rearrange the letters in the name Seti Rousike, you can make the more familiar name, Kuri Osites.

Pages 32-33

To make sense of the dream, you will need to understand the story running through it. The dream mixes fiction and fact. It starts with the twins' father telling them that Skemes built the burial chamber in the wrong place. Then one of the pyramid thieves enters. He must be Klepto Maniak who wrote on the papyrus, as he says that the best of the treasure had already been taken before he got there. One crook leads to another as Bricabrac appears and is told by Inigo Outicombe that the tunnel he's in should be blocked. Duncan pops up announcing that he will be kidnapped soon. Then, a very sinister-looking Iona enters and the dream falls into fantasy. As Iona and Bricabrac claim the treasure as their own, a bandaged mummy makes his appearance. This is presumably Narcemes who clearly says that the treasure is his and that "it always has been". What can this mean? Then the mummy goes back to the perplexing riddle about the middle and where the middle might be. This refers to where the burial chamber is positioned in the pyramid, "deep down in the ground far under the mound? Or in the centre? We'll see . . . Remember – even a Pharaoh can change his mind".

Pages 34-35

Gusto and Duncan are in the locked room, which is the one next to the twins' bedroom (see page 23). Although the ladders and rocks might be useful, the easiest escape route is to climb down the vine outside the window. Gusto knows that the vine reaches to the ground from her escape.

Pages 36-37

Yes. Inigo Outicombe's plan of the pyramid on page 11 shows an air vent running from the top of the main ascending corridor into the descending corridor which leads to the underground chamber.

Use the cipher on page 21 to decode the symbols. Reading downwards from right to left, with spaces and punctuation marks added, this is what they say:

My architect, Skemes, made no mistake,
The chamber above was simply a fake.
This is the real one – look around and see
my coffin and treasures, safe as can be.
Now I lie dying but Skemes lives on,
he'll take my place until he too is gone.
We've split the treasure, great and small,
the best are here, but these aren't all.
The rest will be stored above with
     Skemes
when he's entombed, disguised as
     Narcemes.
Whoever you are who solves this plot,
the treasure is yours, the whole stinking
     lot.
No good to me now, to you it may be.
Use it wisely or throw it in the sea.

These were the last words of the Pharaoh, Narcemes the Fourth.

So, the Pyramid Plot turned out to be a set up from the start. Narcemes had planned the whole thing in league with Skemes. They had always intended to have two burial chambers and to hide the best of the treasure in the lower chamber. This is really the meaning behind the confusing riddle of where the middle might be. When Narcemes died, Skemes took his place – maybe this was why Narcemes seemed to be a "new man" in the last years of his life. Skemes, not Narcemes, is the Mummy in the Museum at Oriac. Look at the X-rays and you will see that the Mummy inside Narcemes' coffin is much smaller than the coffin itself – Skemes must have been shorter than his boss.

Meanwhile, Narcemes was buried along with his treasure in the lower chamber. This is why the treasure was safe for all these years. What nobody realized was that the lower chamber was divided into two parts. The burial chamber was sealed off from the antechamber and it was only because of the bullet fracturing the wall that the treasure was ever found. In the end, what Gusto and Jaz thought was a modern plot of sabotage and deception master minded by Iona and a bunch of crooked builders, turned out to be an ancient plot after all…

Finally…

There is a deliberate mistake in one picture in this book. Can you spot it?

And there's one unsolved mystery. Who do you think began translating the papyrus found inside the broken pot on page 13?

If you think you know the answers, why not write and tell us?

This edition first published in 2001 by Usborne Publishing Ltd., Usborne House, 83-85 Saffron Hill, London EC1N 8RT, England. www.usborne.com Copyright © 2001, 1992 Usborne Publishing Ltd. The name Usborne and the devices ⚑ ⚐ are Trade Marks of Usborne Publishing Ltd. All rights reserved. No part of this publication may be reproduced, stored in a retrieval system or transmitted in any form or by any means, electronic, mechanical, photocopying, recording or otherwise without the prior permission of the publisher. Manufactured in China. U.E.